"Ours is not to reason why...."

Karen

To Lois:

Beyond tomorrow's highlights, we'll look back, remember, and cherish, the thoughts that were never spoken but always understood. Yesterdays unspoken happenings will always be tomorrows fondest memories. But remember do not dwell on the past for all time. you must still prepare yourself for the future's future.

Karen Skillings. May/1976

TOLLER

TOLLER

Elva Oglanby

Illustrations by Toller Cranston

Photographs by David Street

GAGE PUBLISHING LIMITED

Gage Publishing Limited

Designer: Fortunato Aglialoro

ISBN 0-7715-9944-7

Printed and Bound in Canada

2 3 4 5 BP 79 78 77 76

Acknowledgments

The Golden Elk, reproduced by permission of Mrs. R. Higgins

The Strawberry Queen, The Virgin Bride, and *The Last Voyage,* reproduced by permission of Mrs. Ellen Burka

Introduction

He has the face of a granite angel. That he is an artist on canvas is evident when one sees him perform on the ice. His images are so burning, so brilliant, that only when one ceases to try to understand them can one even begin to appreciate the qualities they communicate. He is multi-facetted, dedicated, driven by an incredible flood of creative energy. He is Toller Cranston.

A year ago I became convinced that this extraordinary personality must be captured between the pages of a book. What has evolved is, of necessity, a unique form of biography, a portrait in words and pictures. It is the result of many hours of taped interviews, conversations, personal observations and sometimes plain intuition. For the most part the book consists of extracts from these sources, quoted exactly, because Toller's unusual approach to life is best expressed in his own words. Occasionally I have taken literary licence and dramatized sections of the narrative. The poems and illustrations, of course, are his own. The result is very far from being a definitive study of this complex character. On the contrary, I have only just begun to scratch the surface. I hope the reader will find, as I did, a fascinating insight into a man who is one of the great artists of our time.

My task would have been impossible without the generous co-operation and patient collaboration of Toller himself. He was at all times gracious and helpful, and I would like to thank him sincerely. Also I want to express my gratitude to my photographer, David Street, who added his own special genius to this book. His photographs are brilliantly interpretive and they have added a whole new dimension to the book.

I would also like to thank my good friend, Marilyn Martin, for her suggestions and advice; my husband, Bill, for his constant patience and help; and my two sons, Andrew and Struan, for their inspiration. I can only hope that their minds will always have wings.

Elva Oglanby
Toronto
September 5, 1975

'Stars in a delirious sky gleam
and go out, and you, sweet artist,
you and I, we too must die, we
too must die.'

Aldous Huxley

Artists are the tools of God. They are driven mercilessly towards goals they are powerless to alter. They are the instruments of destiny. Their lives are not their own.

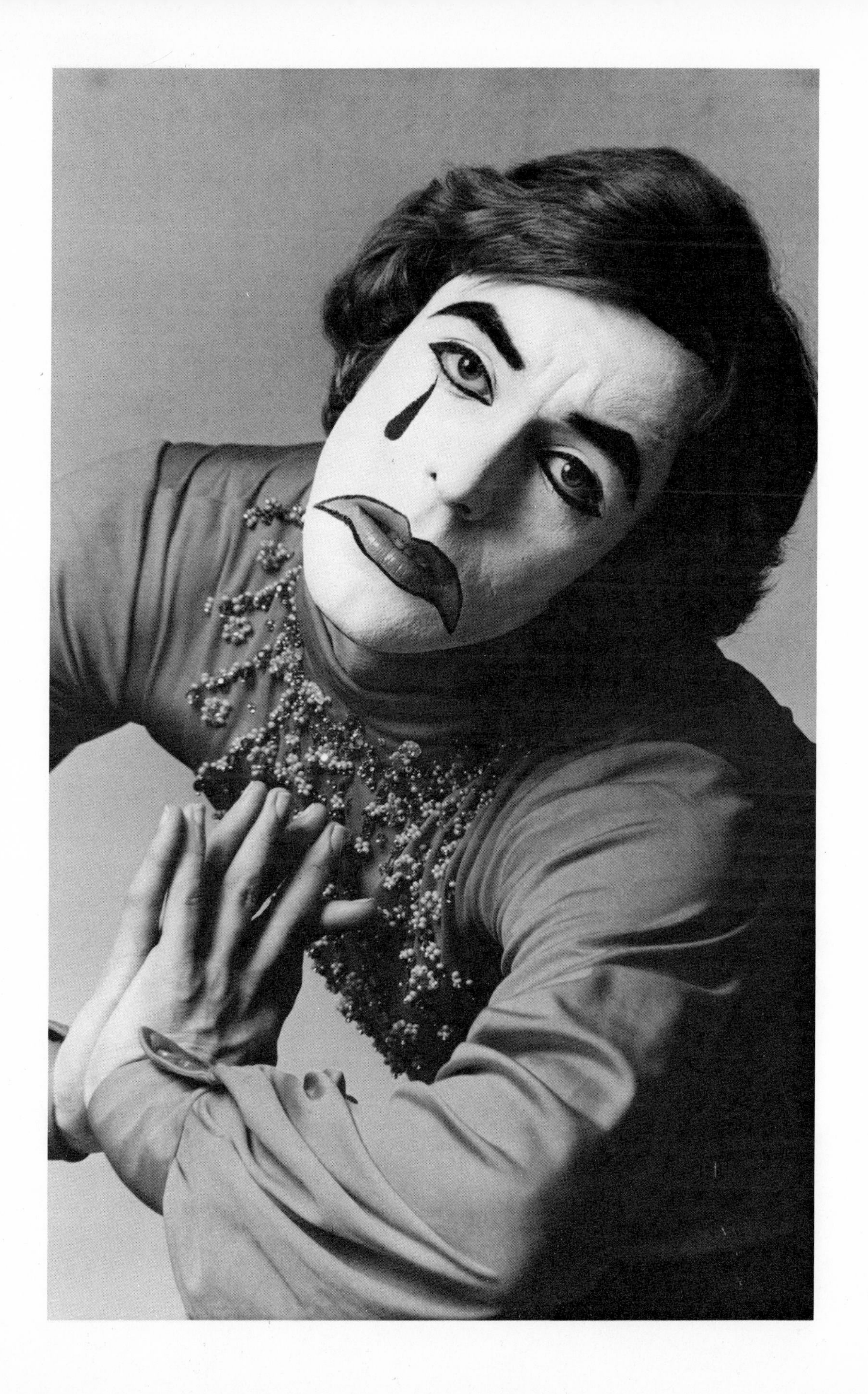

The most important statement I have ever made in skating, I made through *I Pagliacci*. Leoncavallo's tragic clown echoes the small, sad voice of humanity, and when I brought the opera to the ice, it was the beginning of a whole new era in my skating and in my life. A door had opened.

I remember the night *Pagliacci* was created. I felt that strange excitement that comes when you know you are on the verge of something special. A breakthrough. From the moment the music began to pervade my body, the program seemed to fall into place. It was all there as though some divine hand had already blocked it out for me. Normally I am very much aware of the other skaters at the club, but this particular night I was oblivious to them all. I shut them out of my mind. Even though the program was still in its most primitive stages, they cleared the ice for me. They seemed to realize what was happening. A Felliniesque touch was added to the occasion when a wedding party noticed us through the glass. The festivities came to an abrupt halt as the bride and the groom and sixty guests came down to the edge of the rink to watch. They stood there for a long time, and many of them had tears in their eyes.

Munich was a fitting choice for the debut of *I Pagliacci.* In the World Championships I had had a disastrous showing in the school figures but had won the free-skate section. I had finished third overall. It was vital for me to do something in the exhibition that would leave an indelible impression on this most sophisticated of audiences. The night before the exhibition I went down to the practice rink to go over the *Pagliacci* program, and I was stunned to find more than 2,000 people inside the arena. There was an awesome hush over everything, an expectancy. It was as though all those people were holding their breath, waiting . . .

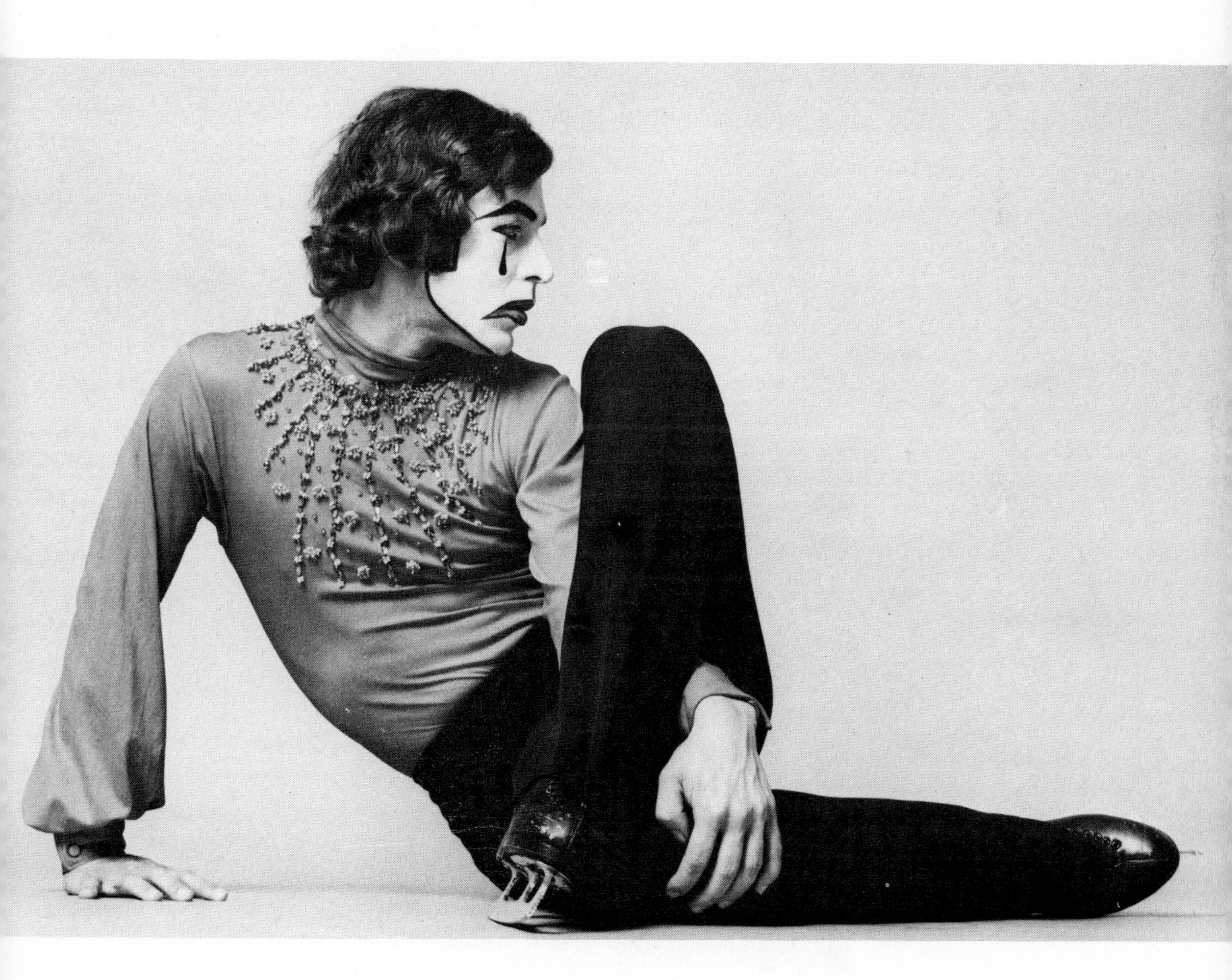

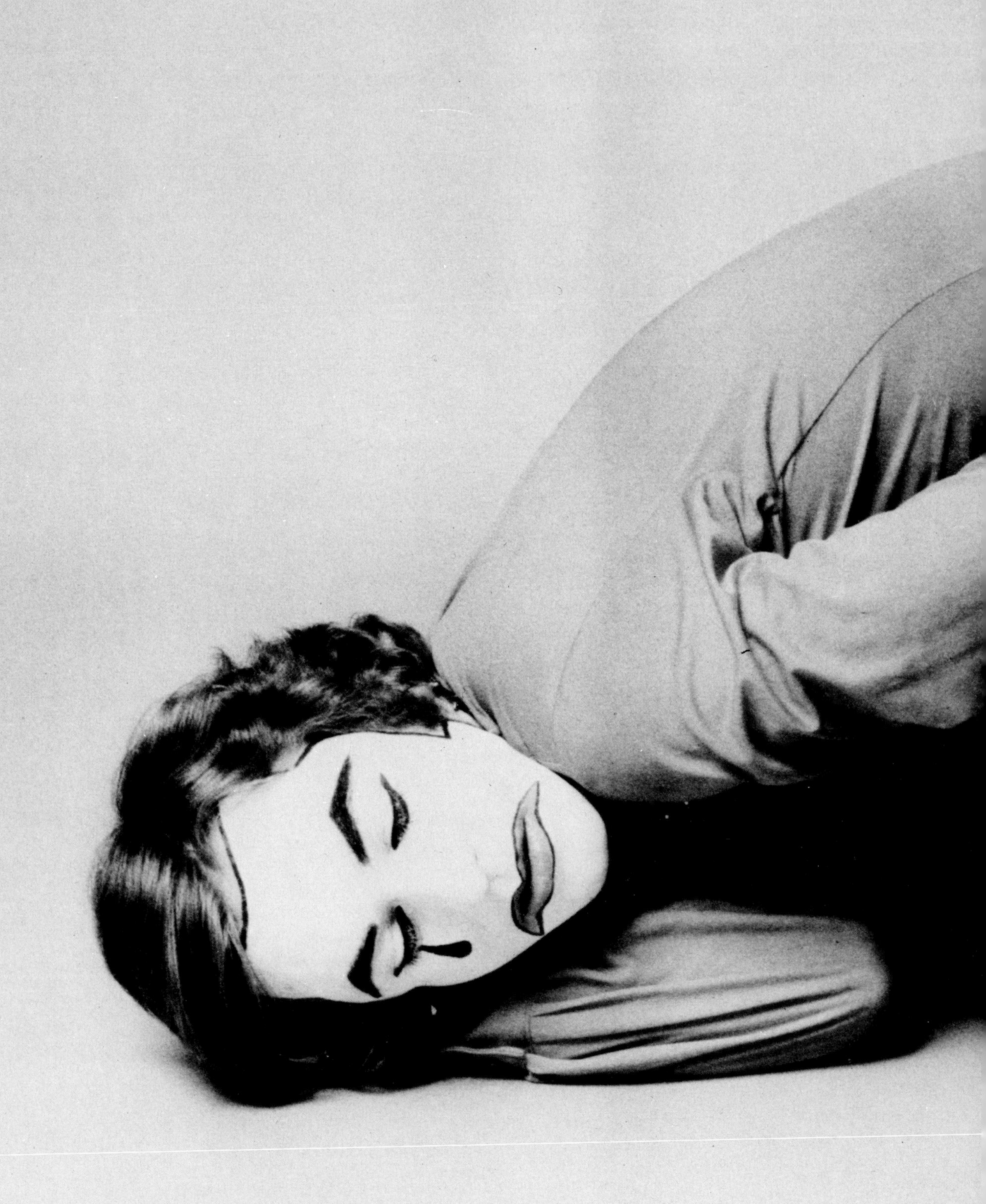

Finally the time came for the performance. The Olympia Halle was crowded to capacity. The audience was still, watching intently, anticipating. As Canio's laugh rang out of the darkness, I felt an electric shock run through the crowd. They understood. In that brief instant we fused. Reality no longer existed and time became suspended. We opened the gateway to tomorrow that night and passed through. We could feel it; we could feel the birth pangs. It was something beyond love, beyond reality. We had entered the fourth dimension, and now all things were possible.

Your tears
Speak to me.

Your words
Are silent spears
Which pierce the fragile
Fabric of my yesteryears.

I always thought I was the only person in the whole world born on April 20, until I discovered that Adolf Hitler was too. Had I been allowed to choose the day on which to be born, April 20 is exactly the day I would have chosen. It is right on the cusp of Aries and Taurus, the one place in the entire zodiac where two very strong signs collide. My friends say I have been blessed (my enemies say cursed) with characteristics from both of those signs. Aries is athletic, strong, persuasive, and overpowering. Taurus is stubborn, creative, and always sure he's right. What an invincible combination, but how exhausting. Yet I would never have wished it any other way. If I were asked which sign I favored, I would have to say Aries, because I am definitely more ram than bull.

I was born, just for the record, at 6:20 a.m. in Hamilton General Hospital, the second of the Cranston children. I had been preceded by my sister Phillippa, and was later to be followed by twin brothers, Goldie and Guy. Their birth is something I still remember, for we were dispatched to the house of my grandparents to await their arrival. In those days our grandparents' house seemed like a castle, and we explored it happily until the time came for us to return home to meet our brothers. We had been told that there were twins and that we each would get one to look after, but it wasn't until we saw the tiny forms lying in the bassinets that we realized they were alive.

My mother has always been intensely creative. She has a hunger for adventure that is reflected in everything she does. The tragedy of her life was that, as a child, she was never encouraged to develop her artistic potential and, as an adult, the demands of raising four children left her little time to concentrate on creative outlets. She is highly literate and an entertaining conversationalist, and she passed on to us children a love of fantasy that has proved to be the mainstay of my life.

My father is a quiet and unassuming man whose only aim in life is to love and provide for his family. He is the gentlest and kindest man in the whole world, and I always grieved that I was unable to be the kind of son to him that he deserved.

My sister is a kind of free spirit, creative in her own way, definitely not run-of-the-mill. We got on really well together as small children, became deadly enemies as older children, and later mellowed into friendly strangers. My brothers I never really knew.

Toller was not an easy child to raise. At times he drove us to the point of insanity—he was so self-willed and determined to have his own way. Yet from the time he was able to talk we knew he was a special person. We realized he was gifted. Our biggest problem was in trying to contain him long enough for him to grow up.

His mother

I never really understood Toller—I still don't. But I love him dearly and I am so very proud of him. Sometimes I despair that there is nothing I can do to help him, but he just won't let me come close to him. He has always been that way. Out there on his own.

His father

As I look back across my life, it appears to me in scattered fragments, stray images too elusive to be catalogued exactly. I was born old, was never really what is called a child. My early years were not a time of carefree joy but rather a time of waiting out the storm until I could arrive. I was very detached from other children. I never could identify with any of them. It was a constant effort for me to pretend to like the things they liked. I could never understand their games—cowboys and Indians and cops and robbers were nightmares. I was much more at home with paints and crayons. At Christmas I would inevitably be presented with a profusion of trucks and cars and other things intended to delight a small boy. Then I would spend a most frustrating day pretending to play with them, simulating the appropriate noises, until the hour came when the donors would mercifully depart for home, and I could put the offending toys away.

When we were very young my sister and I had a liking for small china ornaments, our first *objets d'art*. I distinctly remember one Christmas when Santa made a terrible mistake and put into the toe of my stocking the china gnome intended for my sister. I was overjoyed to discover I had been given two and was convinced that Santa had divined my superior ability to cherish them. My mother, on the other hand, was distraught at the injustice and snatched the gnome from my hand to give it to my sister. I secretly wrote a tearful letter to Santa to tell him of the outrage, but he must have been too busy to reply.

When we were small we moved about frequently. Because of this we were never quite sure of our position in society. When we moved into the house near Kirkland Lake, however, we believed that we had found the answer. We were millionaires. In our fireplace there was a rock which contained a vein of pure gold. Eagerly we took every new visitor to view the evidence of our status. To our childish eyes the house was a mansion. It had a large garden, completely surrounded by a fence with two gates. Inside the fence was a strawberry patch and a wishing well. I would spend many hours beside the wishing well in innocent futility, wishing for a best friend or a dog. Neither ever came. There was a tower the walls of which were studded with pieces of colored glass. To us children they were the rarest jewels, and we would take great delight in prying them out. Pieces of dark blue Noxzema glass were always the most coveted. I was five or six when we moved there, and on the whole it was a good time in my life.

As a small child I possessed an insatiable curiosity. I would spend many hours in deep discussion with adults and many more hours completely alone inside my own head. I took the greatest delight in shocking people, and I was forever getting into trouble.

We were always having to bail Toller out. Once, when he was three years old—we were living in Galt at the time—we had a call from the police station to go and retrieve him. We had thought he was safely in bed. It was a dreadful night pouring with rain. When we arrived at the police station, there was Toller calmly sitting wearing nothing at all except his father's galoshes. He had taken my umbrella and decided to go for a walk.

His mother

My artistic inclinations also tended to get me into trouble. The earliest example I can remember is the day my sister and I dug up the front lawn of our house in Galt. We made a miniature Stonehenge and thought it was magnificent. When our parents found it, however, they were furious. We never could understand why.

Another constant source of friction was my desire to perform in public. Mother often would have gatherings in the house and I loved nothing better than to shed my shoes and dance on my bare toe points. The people watching would grind their teeth in horror, and I adored the notoriety. It inevitably ended with my being put to bed, and I would lie there seething with rage at the injustice of the world, and plotting my revenge.

I was strongly attracted to pure colors even as a very small child. Once, I remember, my mother was invited to pick some flowers at the home of a horticulturist while the lady was away on vacation. Mother was delighted, and at the first opportunity she drove us all to the house to cut some blooms. The very second the car stopped — even before — I leaped out and rushed like lightning across to where a vast dahlia was growing beside the front door. It was yellow, the most magnificent blazing yellow I had ever seen, and I knew that was the flower I wanted. It had an enormous head that must have weighed all of three pounds and was the size of a soup plate. I grabbed the stem and pulled, and the head snapped off. My mother was mortified and immediately threw me and my stolen treasure back into the car and drove off before anyone could see what I had done. I had chosen to pluck the dahlia the woman was growing for the local garden fair. The irony of the whole thing was that mother floated the head in a giant soup tureen, and everyone admired it and said it was fabulous. But I wasn't spoken to for a whole week.

People tend to view me as true blue and beyond reproach, and that bothers me. Nobody in the world is beyond reproach. I think I committed my first real crime at the age of six. There was a river near our house, where ducks used to nest. Ducks and Canada geese. In the spring the children would go down and feed them. One particular spring day my mother gave us some breadcrumbs, and we went to the riverbank to give them to the birds. We had been warned repeatedly about the birds nesting, and yet for some reason I intentionally broke a duck's egg. I stepped on it, only to discover with horror that the fetal duck had almost hatched. How could I have done such a thing, when all the ducks had nested there, trusting us? And yet, even in my guilt, I distinctly recall the delicious satisfaction I got as I scrunched that egg; the moment of power that I experienced. But it was short-lived. I was in deadly terror of the other children reporting me to the police. For weeks afterward every footstep behind me had a definite military ring.

My most terrifying memory concerns a dog. It still sends shivers down my spine to think about it. I was seven at the time. One morning during recess I wandered alone along the fence around the school yard. The snow was packed against it in hard, crisp piles, and the cold was intense — lung-searing, breath-fogging cold. I climbed on top of a pile of snow and rested my head against the fence idly wondering what cold iron tasted like. I put out my tongue to lick the icy bar and it immediately stuck fast. I was stricken with terror. I could not pull it off. As I crouched there helplessly in the snow I noticed a dog devouring a ghastly-looking carcass, tearing it to bits. I became hysterical and began to shriek, and because I startled him, the dog turned round and bit me right through my snowsuit. I was so terrified that I ripped my tongue right off the fence, leaving behind part of the skin, and ran home screaming to my mother. Blood was gushing down the front of my snowsuit, and it took two hours before I could be calmed.
I made such a fuss that my mother called the police about the dog. When I went back to school that same afternoon, I distinctly remember seeing the dog being dragged by the scruff of his neck toward the woods by a policeman in elbow-length leather gloves. All of us kids turned out to watch him go, and as he passed us the little mongrel turned his head for just a fraction of a second to look at me. He looked at me so accusingly, so steadily, that I squirmed under his gaze. And when they disappeared into the woods and the shot rang out in the still winter air, the other kids turned to me and pointed accusing fingers at me. "You did that to that little dog," they said. "*You* did that." And even though I protested that it was because

the dog had bitten me, I felt utterly wretched. For the first time in my life I had felt the full weight of responsibility, and I was ashamed.

I have no clear recollection of beginning school. All I know is that I never particularly cared for it. It was a succession of classes, of unimportant goals that had to be achieved. And were. Some God-given instinct guided me through those years with a certain hand. Otherwise I might still be faced with the unsupportable task of completing Grade 12. My path through school was not, however, smooth. At times it was distinctly stormy.

By the time I was in the eighth grade, my sister Phillippa and I did not communicate at all. For us to attempt even the most basic civilities was only to trigger off a deadly row. I owned at the time a splendid stuffed cobra, which I had purchased from Lady Lane's gift shop near our house in Montreal. It was my supreme weapon against Phillippa. She lived in mortal terror of reptiles, and I would arrange the offending creature so that its head was poking out the door of my bedroom. It always produced exquisite hysteria in her, exactly as I planned. One day, however, the cobra was accidently lanced through the neck, and it bled sawdust all over the carpet. It was then retired to the interior of a paper bag, and relegated to the back of my bedroom cupboard, where it lay dormant for weeks. Everyone forgot about it, until one day, our cleaning lady, known to us as "Moany" Meucis, unwittingly unveiled it again. Her habitual moans built into a magnificent crescendo of wails, shrieks, and howls, and she was taken home in a taxi and never seen again. Neither, for that matter was the cobra.

Long, long before I had ever heard of skating, I wanted to be a dancer. I was obsessed by the desire and could think of little else. To my absolute joy, when I was five years old, I was allowed to attend ballet classes with my sister. My life was set, or so I believed, the first time I boarded the bus for the dance studio. I was going to become a great dancer. My dream, my precious bubble, lasted exactly thirty minutes. I was an immediate failure, unable to keep time with the other children, mixing left foot with right, bored to distraction with the exercises at the barre. I was devastated and never went back.

At the age of seven I was taken to see my sister skate in her first carnival. The moment I saw her I knew I wanted to skate too. I had a new obsession. The following year I was allowed to have lessons, and seven months later I made my show skating debut in the Kirkland Lake carnival. I wanted to be an immediate sensation, so I worked and worked until I could do a Cossack routine — the one where you crouch on your heels and shoot your legs out in front, one after the other. I mastered it so well that the crowd gave me a standing ovation. They roared for more. In the middle of the ice I burst into tears, because I had prepared no encores.

As a child I had delusions of grandeur believing our ancestors to have descended from the bluest Scottish blood. To my utter devastation I learned that the Cranston clan had, in fact, stemmed from a long line of notorious smugglers, bandits, and thieves.

Great Auntie My was the only member of the Cranston clan for whom I felt a great affinity. She was known as Great Auntie Swingpants. She was the only true eccentric in our whole family, and she lived in New York City. The presents she would send to us each Christmas were unwrapped with a great sense of foreboding. One never knew what one might get. When I was six I received one hundred tea bags; at seven I struck it rich with a silver beer mug; and when I was eight I received an enormous nutbowl full of hazelnuts. The family was aghast but I was overjoyed. That same Christmas my gigantic nutbowl was rather overshadowed when my sister unwrapped her gift. She received the splendid sum of twenty used metallic hairnets.

Once I had a dream about death — the kind of dream you waken from unsure any longer of what is real and what is fantasy. In my dream, death was neither grotesque nor terrifying. It was actually rather peaceful. We were all little children again, mounted on the great dragon of death, maturity stripped from us like clothing we no longer needed. We floated, cautious perhaps, trusting certainly, for what else do little children do but trust? Decisions were no longer ours to make. We were faced at last with the fact of inevitability, and our search was over.

When I was fourteen I tried to take my life. It is not an action I am proud to recall. It was a stupid and senseless thing to do. All I can remember is lying on my bed and swallowing a great quantity of Bufferins. I fell into a deep and dreamless sleep from which I never expected to awaken, but the next morning I woke up feeling, if anything, slightly better than I normally do first thing in the morning. I lay there for a while experiencing a mixture of shame and relief, and all I could think of was how hungry I was. I shall never try it again. I am quite certain of that. Life is too full of possibilities.

Ever since I can remember, women have been the central figures in my life. When I was three we had a baby-sitter called Mrs. Tyler. She was comfortably middle-aged and she adored me. She would knit me very special socks and sweaters. I would talk to Mrs. Tyler by the hour, and we developed a mutual rapport. Alas, the idyll was not to last. One particular night my parents returned home from an evening out to discover Mrs. Tyler had been nipping at the Scotch and had become inebriated. Poor Mrs. Tyler wept and pleaded eternal sobriety if she could be given one more chance. My father propelled her into the car and drove her home. She never came again.

Miss Linton was the first real friend I ever had. I met her in the park one day when I was five years old. In that strange way that these things sometimes happen, we recognized each other straightaway. It is difficult for me to recall her face, yet she left her mark upon my life. We met almost daily in a nearby park — the frail old lady and the small boy. One day she invited me back to her apartment to have tea. She had things in there which intrigued me endlessly, and I explored them all. The most hallowed place of all was her attic, in which stood an ancient trunk filled with the effects of

her dead brother. He had lived in the Far East, and Miss Linton told me that in the trunk was a bejewelled kimono, a treasure which I longed to see. Each time I waited for her in the park, I fantasized that she would come garbed in the treasured robe but she never did. The night before we moved to Montreal, I was allowed to take Miss Linton out for dinner on my own. It was a very special occasion for each of us. I never saw her again after that although we wrote occasionally. Then one day I heard that she was dead. That very night she came to see me in a dream, although I had never dreamed of her before. I dreamed of her often after that.

Eva Vasak was my first real trainer. When I was ten we moved to Montreal, to Baie D'Urfée, and the second day I was there I travelled to Lachine by bus with my sister to skate at the arena. The following day, when my mother came down to arrange for lessons, Eva Vasak approached her and asked to be allowed to teach me. She had watched me the night before and had seen something in my skating that she found exciting. For the eight years that she taught me she refused any payment for my lessons and gave me everything she knew. I was like a son to her. She was the first person ever to see the artistic potential in my skating, and she nurtured that seed and cultivated it lovingly. Finally, she urged me to leave her and go to Toronto. She knew that if I stayed in Montreal I would never make the Canadian team. It broke her heart, but she insisted that I go.

Madame Daoust was one of the most generous women I have ever known. The day I started at the École des Beaux Arts in Montreal, I went to the office to pay my registration fees. I offered them a cheque but they wouldn't accept it. Madame Daoust was the superintendent there, and she said to me, "Don't worry, I'll pay the fees for you. You can pay me back tomorrow." When I came in the next day with the money, she wouldn't take it from me. She just smiled at me and said, "Don't bother paying me back. I am delighted to help. But when you get the chance, do the same for someone else."

Certain people are woven through your life like threads. Sometimes they will disappear for long periods, but always they are there, underneath the surface. I have scattered memories of the gradual surfacing of one of these special people in my own life. I first met Lady Lane when I was eleven years old. I had gone into her gift shop in Montreal to buy some Christmas presents. Her shop was filled with a profusion of exotic things from all over the world, and the things that fascinated me the most were the stuffed cobras. Lady Lane and I shared a mutual interest in them. She was, and still is, a most remarkable lady. She defies age and has captured the secret of eternal youth. Although she is actually many years older than me, we have become close friends. There is a refinement in her that I find very attractive and a love of adventure that is not abandoned but controlled. There just aren't that many women in the world who would go off completely alone and stomp through the jungles bargaining with head-hunters. Yet she does exactly that and much, much more. She has an endless font of stories to tell, and when I am with her I am never, never bored.

Toller first came into my shop when he was eleven years old. He was a child immediately set apart from other children. It's not easy to say why, except that he had an air of authority about him, a method of making the first attack upon the other person which was apt to disarm one. I remember so well this particular day, just before Christmas, when he came in to buy gifts for his family. I watched him strutting superciliously around the store, examining everything, and he suddenly said, "Tell me, why are all these cobras coiled to the right and none of them to the left?" It was so strange a question for an eleven-year-old to ask, because there was, in fact, a very good reason for the direction of the coiling, but Toller was the first person besides myself who had ever remarked on it. I explained to him that on one of my trips to India I had asked that same question and had been told that cobras only ever veer to the right, never to the left, and that if a person were ever to be attacked by a cobra, they could escape quite easily by darting in the opposite direction. He was most interested in the answer I gave him and went on to ask all kinds of questions, devouring every scrap of information he could get. He was a remarkable conversationalist, not really a child. When finally I suggested some gifts he might buy for his family, he firmly rejected them. I shall never forget his face. "I couldn't possibly afford that much. I have to save most of my money for figure skates. You see, I am going to be Canadian champion one day."

Lady Lane

I'm not sure why it is, but all my best friends have been women. Certainly I prefer to work with them. The best trainers in the world are women; the really great ones have a combination of masculine and feminine qualities. They are lonely women, only finding happiness through their protégées. At its best, it is a fragile form of happiness.

I may not always be right,

but I'm absolutely *never* wrong!

A Ram's Eye View of the Zodiac

ARIES	Pure Gold. *Numero uno.* Follow me, follow me, but never, never touch. I will lead you into the land of everything, but once we get there, I will abandon you.
TAURUS	Bully for the Bronze! Artistic impression high, but technical ability deficient.
GEMINI	Will try everything once but never on a Sunday.
CANCER	Need one say more?
LEO	Theatrical puffballs. All woo and no do.
VIRGO	Never wrong, but also never right. Passable for women and *tragique* for men.
LIBRA	Flexible to the point of elasticity.
SCORPIO	Congratulations, the Silver!
SAGITTARIUS	Amusing in small doses, when behind glass.
CAPRICORN	Oh, dear!
AQUARIUS	Indispensable at weddings and funerals. No organ should be without one.
PISCES	One month premature, but useful to have around.

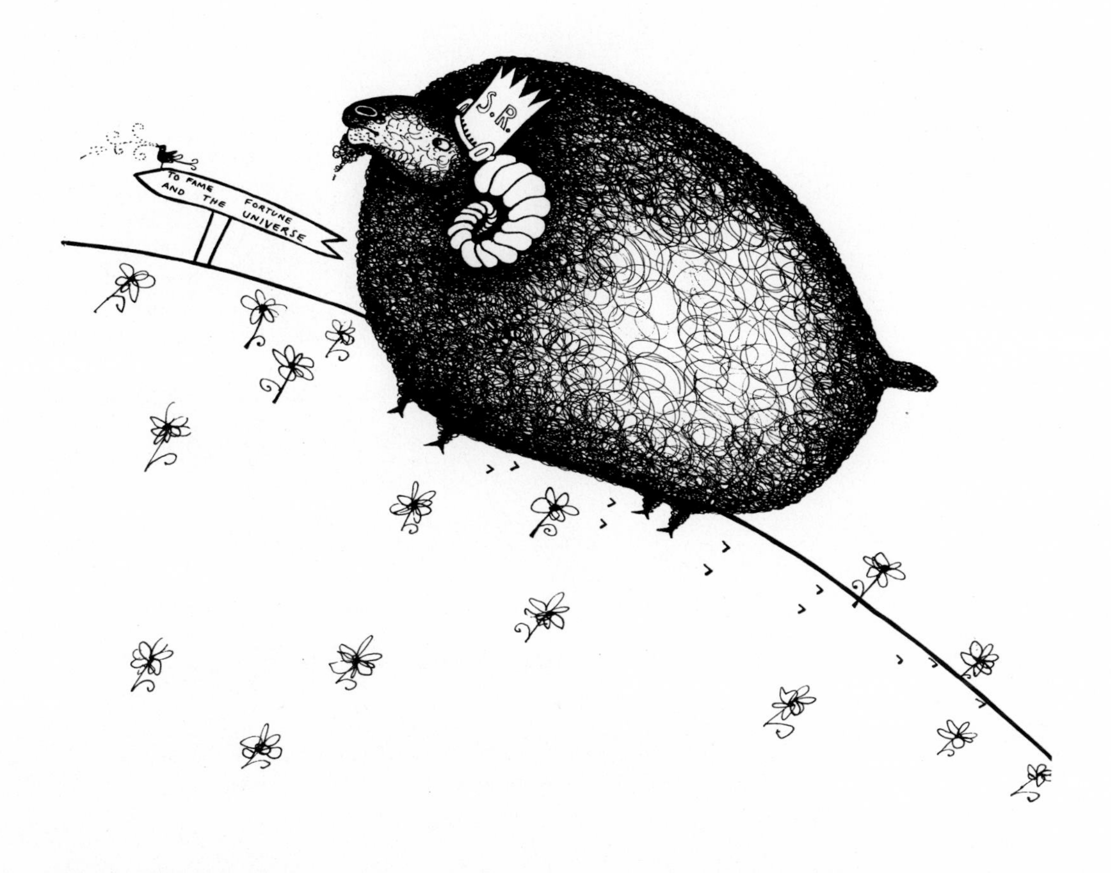

Aries is the only sign under which to be born. It gives one such an advantage in life! A true Aries will never waste time brooding over the fact that what goes up must come down. An Aries will be far too busy making sure that the damned things goes up in the first place.

If an Aries child does not resemble a ram, his mother has made a terrible mistake.

Although Christ was born a Capricorn, given free will he chose to return as an Aries.

If you cannot understand my silences, how can you begin to understand my words?

By the age of six I had been singled out by my family as being artistic, an attribute they acknowledged with a mixture of shame and pride. My mother was the first to recognize the signs in me, and she did her best to encourage them. She taught me all she could.

Even in my earliest years realism in art held no appeal for me. To this day I still dismiss it. From the very first, my work was marked by an utter lack of realism. My paintings, even then, were most unusual, full of intentional design, always strongly stated. Jewel colors and exotic forms fascinated me. I can still recall the first time I was allowed to do an abstract design in class—it was in Grade 2. We were given paper and crayons and told to draw whatever we felt like drawing. I did a magnificently complicated design in bold colors of black, purple, and blue, almost a Paisley design. I knew what it would look like before I even started to work on it. When it was pinned up on the wall with all the others I felt a surge of pride. I knew that it was strong. Yet not one person ever noticed it. My work was never fully understood at school, and I can still feel the sheer frustration of those days.

It was not so very different when I was in high school. I tried to cover up my minor eccentricities and blend in with the other students, but always there was a feeling of frustration.

I only discovered my innermost self when I went to the Ecole des Beaux Arts and found that total strangers were actually members of my tribe. Any eccentricity that I had tried to hide in school was now completely overshadowed by the greater eccentricities of my fellow students. I could relax at last.

When I first began my studies there, I went through a period of despising everyone who was not an art student. We were, I felt, so superior, so free, so talented! I think it must have been a reaction to my high school days when I had never been encouraged to experiment or progress. I had been held in a tight, straight line, and my work had stifled. At the Ecole des Beaux Arts I felt I could accomplish anything, try anything. The lectures and the new people to whom I was exposed affected my whole outlook on life, and I began to see things through new and different eyes. It was an exciting period for me. I was living in an environment where talent reigned supreme.

By far the most brilliant of us all was an Irishman called David Moore. He was a reincarnation of Van Gogh, lit with an inner beauty that transcended everything. He had a gigantic nose, jug-handle ears, thyroid eyes, wild, wiry hair, and one discolored tooth in the centre of his mouth. He lived a life of abject poverty and we idolized him. I remember a girl who had magnificent hair which flowed to the ground and trailed behind her like a train. She was famous for never doing any work, but with hair like that we could forgive her. And another I can still remember was an astonishingly handsome specimen with finely chiselled features and an alabaster skin. He had a crown of fine black hair and was known to have had a flaming affair with his mother. Because of this his wild, unshapen abstracts and maniacal paintings were all accepted and forgiven, and everything was blamed on his father.

I wanted very much to live in a basement like my friends and be chic but had to commute from the suburbs instead. In 1968 I had a gruelling schedule. I would be up at 4 a.m. in order to skate at the Town of Mount Royal arena from 5-9 a.m. Then I would commute to art school. I spent my lunch hour running up twenty-three flights of stairs to try to keep in condition for the Canadian Championships. The first time I did it I fainted at the top! After school I would rush home, eat, rest, and skate from 8-11 p.m. at the Lachine arena. Luckily I have never been a stranger to discipline, and somehow I got through those days.

Not all my lunch hours were spent running up stairs, however. Often friends and I would sneak into Place des Arts and watch whatever was in rehearsal there. We received an entire cultural education this way and saw the best of everything during those three years. Other lunch hours would be spent perusing the books in the library, for the school boasted the largest art library in North America.

By the third year I was beginning to get restless. We seemed to be forever experimenting and never finished anything. I was a better than average student, though not the most outstanding, and one of the youngest there. As a sculptor I was a dire disgrace and rarely ever went to classes. The teacher, Joan Essar, became my friend and understood the way I felt. She always passed me, although my completed projects were few and far between. Eventually I took my work to one of the top teachers, Jacques de Tonnancour, and asked him what I should do. He took his time and then said, "There is nothing more the Ecole des Beaux Arts can do for you. You must get out on your own and paint. Involve yourself in as much work as you can." That was exactly what I wanted to hear and I never went back.

I Have Always Wanted

to hear Judy Garland sing, but I'll have to save her for another lifetime

be the lower half of a death spiral

purge myself in the Ganges

be invisible

explore the interior of the pyramids

get inside another person's mind

live in a houseboat in Kashmir

eat ice cream from a golden brick

drown in a sea of schmaltz

ask Napoleon what Josephine was like in bed

encounter Shangri-La

Shadow
Long years ago
I used to call your name
And ask you
Why are you there?
Is this a game
You play?
Please let me in.

Butterfly soft
You sat on my shoulder
Holding my breath
Waiting
For me to notice you.
You knew I would.

Shadow
When I was young
I still believed you were
A part of me.
Trust was the air I breathed
And not a word.
But when I turned around
To smile at you
Just like the others
You were gone.

Every time the human fusion splits the darkness with its first sharp cry, man asks again the primal question—why?

I feel mortality's cold hand and death a passing sigh, and ask again why does the seed of my own manhood contain the embryonic echo of myself?

I wish I knew.

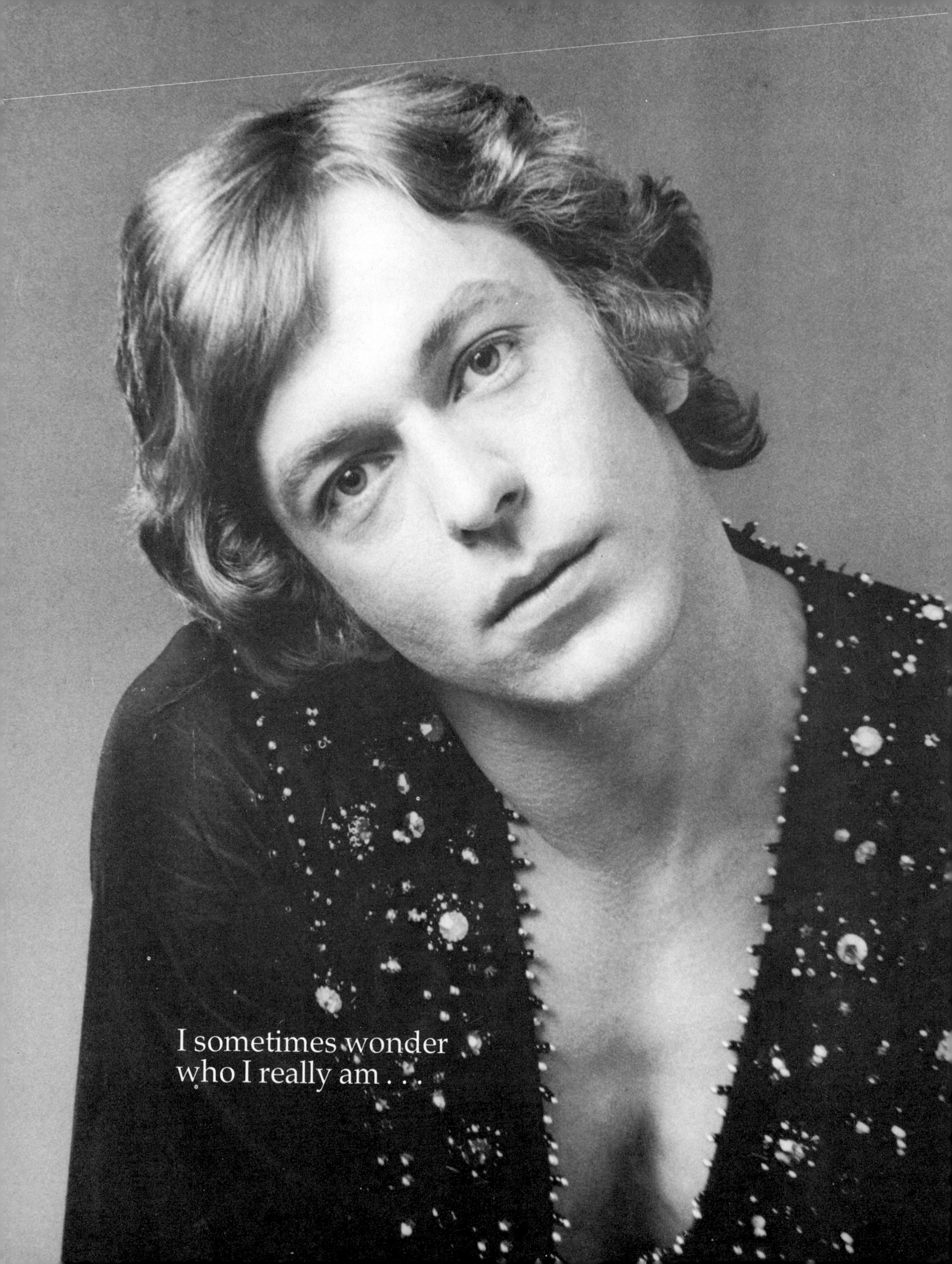
I sometimes wonder
who I really am . . .

A hundred voices clamor inside me
calling in so many different ways

Even my reflection contradicts

The only thing I can be certain of . . .
. . .is that my name is Toller.

My demented endeavors while at the Ecole des Beaux Arts to keep myself in shape were aimed at the Canadian Championships in Vancouver and a place on the 1968 Olympic team. I drove myself mercilessly. When the time came to compete I placed fifth in school figures. I was the last skater to skate the free-skate, and, although everything in my body said no, my mind was crying yes. I skated like a madman. I was chasing a place on the team that was not intended to be mine and gave it everything I had. No audience has ever given me a greater reception, and as the music stopped they came to their feet. In my heart, although I knew it was impossible, I believed I had pulled it off. When the marks came up I saw that I was wrong. There was an eleven point spread. The judges had not understood my skating. The audience was angry. I came off the ice like a zombie keeping my eyes wide open, so that the tears would not come. They spilled out anyway, and right at that moment I met Mrs. Burka, who was later to become my trainer and my friend. She took me by the arm and pulled me into a small room off the arena. She said, "Stop crying. Go out there again and meet them with your head up high. Be proud, because you are the most artistic skater in the world." That competition marked the beginning of a controversy that has raged around my performances for years, but I have never wept for skating since.

The fall of 1969 saw me in Lake Placid. I lived in a garage and paid for my training by looking after the grounds at the Mirror Lake Inn. Part of my income was free food, and I took full advantage of it. I gained more than twenty pounds, and by September I was in the worst shape of my entire career. Everything pointed to my giving up skating altogether, but one last little flame still burned deep inside me. I remembered Mrs. Burka. She was Canada's top conditioner and was the only person I could think of who could save me. I desperately needed the discipline she offered. I knew she worked at the Toronto Cricket Club, and one night I took my future in my hands and phoned her. I asked her in a trembling voice if she would take me on. Her answer was almost distant: 'Yes, come, but don't expect too much.' I left everything behind and came to Toronto immediately. I was very much alone and was dreadfully unhappy. In four weeks I was thrown out of four boarding houses. My paints made too much mess and the smell offended people. One night I brought my portfolio to the rink and Mrs. Burka was impressed by what she saw. She invited me to stay with her until I found another place. Seven years later I was still there . . .

Lapis is only a dog, but he is one of the most important persons in my life. He is a kind and gentle English setter, intelligent and sage, and without question he is a gift from God. He is only three years old, yet he is part of the fabric of my life.

One cold and wet November night a large wooden crate arrived at the house, and we had it carried through into the kitchen. There was no sound from within. When the door was removed Lapis came out quietly, wagging his tail, accepting us completely. To this day his character remains the same. He never wavers. He loves every human being and every other dog he meets, and I have never heard him growl.

In the unreal life of a competitor, love affairs are virtually impossible. All my affections, therefore, are channelled into Lapis, and he returns them a thousandfold. I often think my sanity depends on him. When competition time draws near and tempers flare, he is my pacifier. Life without him now would be unthinkable.

Inhibition is the deadly enemy of all performers. It places limitations upon their art so that they are never truly great. Something is held back—the results are never total. I had not realized the extent to which I was inhibited until one night at a party I really let myself go. I danced a gypsy dance and poured my soul into what I was doing. I forgot the other people in the room —I was in a world all my own. I astonished everyone. Someone said to me, "You idiot! Why don't you skate that way? It would be sensational!" And that's exactly what I did. I never have been inhibited since then, not even the slightest bit. You only have to do it once. After that it becomes quite easy . . . there is no need to be afraid.

A Year

JULY

A new year. The start of eight weeks intensive summer training. Groundwork is laid for the coming year. Programs set. Techniques improved. No travel allowed. No exhibitions. Nothing. Hours off the ice are spent painting. Art show paintings are begun. Some precious sunny hours are spent sketching on the porch. The sky above is lattice-worked with leaves and small bugs dot my board.

AUGUST

Painting almost impossible. Energy is channelled ruthlessly into training. Everything gives way before the pressures of the schedule. Fatigue is numbing every muscle, every limb. Sleep is now a luxury I can't afford. Music is my closest friend. I travel to Vancouver for the singles seminar where sixty skaters gather for two weeks. Intensive training under Canada's top pros. The minds and bodies are in tune. A time of growth. At the end, five precious days of rest. I find a place to hide away and paint.

SEPTEMBER

Back home again. Another phase begins. A different kind of work. Hard physical conditioning. The body must be fit enough to stand the rigors of a five-minute program. Horrific task but there is no escape. The worst time of the year. There is little chance for painting but I take time in the park. Lapis loves to chase the squirrels.

OCTOBER

A very busy month. Costumes are designed. Fabric is bought. Beading done. Skate Canada draws near. The first competition of the year. The stage is set, the curtain rises. Now is the time for painting once again. A few quiet hours spent off the ice. The first international exhibition. A day or two in Vienna before returning home.

NOVEMBER

Training continues. Skate the Jimmy Fund. Boston looks quite lovely in the fall. Demands increase at home. Time is already overbooked. Requests from radio and television. A visit from the press. A lightning trip to Europe for a combined art/skating exhibition. No time left over for social life. There are times when I would simply like to see a movie with a friend.

DECEMBER

German exhibitions. A new peak at Skate Moscow. If only I had time to linger there. Back home for the taping of the annual Christmas television show at Toronto City Hall. Christmas Day, a hallowed day of rest from everything. (If it ever fell on Sunday I would feel robbed!) I eat too much. December 26 and a new period begins. Training accelerated.

JANUARY

The pace increases. Regional competitions provide a chance to air new programs. Iron out mistakes. The Canadian Championships draw near. Momentum gathers. I dare not miss a single hour on the ice. Painting can be done, but only late at night. Pressures mount. Nerves tighten. Tempers flare. Nothing is more vital than this first major competition. Everything I stand for is at stake. Each year it gets a little harder as the expectations grow. It must be done again against all odds. Success here means a giant boost to international competitions. But this is only the beginning.

FEBRUARY

A time of great financial strife. Preparations must be made before leaving for World's. Two months away from home is difficult. Dog-sitters must be found. Bills prepaid. Costumes must be made and others cleaned. So many extra things. It feels as though I'll never get away. Such great relief to board the plane at last. This is the prelude to the battle, yet I feel a sense of freedom and release. A two-week training camp brings the team together. Everyone is under massive strain and nerves are frayed. The tension breaks at last and helps to clear the air.

MARCH

The final days. A time of inner strength. Only the competition is important now. A whole year's work will be at stake. Triumphs, telegrams, and tears are the hallmarks of the week. The climax brings relief. Medals are won and lost. The tour of champions begins, visiting every major city. Skaters excel and peaks are reached. Brilliant exhibitions. We are at peace. We do not have to think. We drift.

APRIL

The tour continues. Each night brings new emotions. We are all so close together having fun. Standing ovations happen every day. Applause is long. Heady nectar for the hungry bees. Art supplies are bought and each day work is done. I am never more at peace. April 20 comes around and I age a year. I celebrate, though quietly, at home. Every ram must have his day.

MAY

I have to skate several exhibitions. But there is a little time to paint and walk the dog. The year's art plans are made. Lithographs and reproductions must be done. A frantic round of functions to attend.

JUNE

At last the year is ending. Scattered exhibitions still demand attention. A period of painting and deep thoughts. Slowly reality returns. Now is the time to fall in love again.

I went down to the rink this morning to do school figures, but I was so tired that I accomplished next to nothing. I couldn't wait to drag myself back to the house, which is for me a haven, a refuge, a sanctuary. I can't seem to gather enough strength to go downtown and see to all the things I need to do. I much prefer it here. I don't have to face anyone or make decisions. So many artists feel exactly the same way. They wrap security around themselves like a blanket and bury themselves in their work. There are days when I simply turn off and can't be Toller Cranston any more.

In the afternoon I go back to the rink again. I persuade myself that my failure is psychologically induced, something I can control and overcome. The ice is virgin-smooth, unscarred. I am capable of anything — everything. I have to try that triple jump again. Over and over I fall, missing the same jump that yesterday had seemed so easy. But not today. Finally I leave the ice in dark despair. I am not — I will never be — invincible.

Wings are not only for birds; they are also for minds

Well, he's kind of nice. He has smiley eyes. I like the way he laughs. He wanted to see my art work. I didn't really want to show him—he's so good and all himself—but he said please and so I did. I showed him the best one first, the sailboat I did in gold. It took me hours. He looked at it and said, "Oh, dear," and I knew he didn't like it. He didn't like the flowers either. He said, "Perfect," but it sounded like he was saying, "Yuck." And we both looked at the flowers and started to giggle because they did look kind of silly. Then I showed him my most terrible thing of all. It was a picture of a horse flying over the moon. And would you believe it—he liked it? He really did! He sat right up and put his arm around me and said, "Now *this* is good." And he sounded like he meant it. He said, "Green is my favorite for horses too."

A ten year old

There is a caterpillar crawling across my bed. A small, green, juicy thing. Does he ever consider his narrow world? Interpret or accept? How deliciously restful merely to accept. To bury oneself in the warm, safe pillow of inertia. And yet how dull. How utterly claustrophobic to live within the confines of an amniotic mind. Death before life. I am suddenly seized with a hatred of the vile thing and exterminate it instantly.

I definitely don't care for religion as such; I'm quite sure God doesn't either.
As a child I didn't hate church but, rather, bitterly resented the gray flannel shorts I was forced to wear each Sunday. I would be propelled protestingly to church hoping nobody would see me, trying to be invisible. I never quite forgave God for that indignity.

I have to be surrounded by other people and to know that they are there if I need them. I live in dread of being completely isolated. I am not as strong as Gaugin, who went off to the South Seas and was not afraid to be by himself. He knew he was a great painter, and he felt no need to prove it to anybody else.

Once, when I was desperately in need of money, a friend commissioned a painting for her new apartment. I worked like a demon and finished it in record time. All that remained was for the picture to dry, and I racked my brain for ways to speed up the lengthy process. I decided to use my oven. Some time later, as I was talking on the phone, an acrid odor filled the room. The voice at the other end of the line came to a confused halt as I screamed, "I have to go. I have a painting in the oven and I think it's burning!" And indeed it was. I snatched it out and threw it in the sink. Three weeks' work. The flames gave way to giant blisters gyrating horribly beneath the paint. I stared in shattered disbelief. I became hysterical. Later, when I could bring myself to look again, I found the blisters had subsided. The painting miraculously looked better than before, a many-textured masterpiece. The buyer was delighted and I received a flood of orders. Of course I had to turn them down. Inspired work like that cannot be done to order.

I Am Afraid

of redwing blackbirds in the spring
experiencing love, the fairy-tale variety, the kind that everybody always talks about
not experiencing love, the fairy-tale variety, the kind that everybody always talks about
envelopes with windows in them
picking up the phone, because there are always obligations on the other end
being deprived of my hearing and, therefore, of my music
snakes except when they are stuffed
being run over by a car
dentists: but I always go, because I'm even more afraid of losing all my teeth
crowds except when they are watching me
being lonely, but not of being alone
myself

Do you ever weep for me
In the silence of your heart?

Does your smile
Hide a sweet sadness
In your soul?

Will I ever know you?
Do you even know yourself?
Or are you just
Afraid of me?

Sometimes I despair at the enormous inadequacy of words. To communicate only with words one is always at the mercy of one's listener. One says, "Do you understand what I mean?" and the other person answers earnestly, "Oh, I do! I do!" And the heart rages because it can never be certain. So few people are truly articulate that words have become a dubious form of communication. Life asks so many questions that can be answered only through the emotions. How much more certain is the language of the eyes, the heart, the hands — the whole quality of a presence. Even tears can be the answer to a question. I speak to people through my art and through my skating in a way I could never speak to them with words.

Sometimes it is the greatest fun simply to disappear. To go somewhere completely by yourself and not let anyone in the whole world know where you are. I once did that when I was on my way home from Germany. I had to stop over in London for the better part of a day. Instead of checking my bags at the airport and going to see an art gallery or a museum, as I would normally have done, I took a taxicab to the best hotel in London. Once there I checked into the most expensive room they had, dropped every stitch of my grubby clothing onto the floor and spent the whole day nude, taking many delicious baths, watching television, reading the bluest books I had been able to find, and ordering room service every half hour whether I wanted it or not. The sheets were sinfully white, and I spent the entire day — when I was not submerged in the bath — in bed. I plan to do it often.

I used to believe when I was a child that I could fly. I had not heard of Leonardo da Vinci, so my belief was not something inspired by him. One particular day, when I was the proud possessor of a pair of partridge wings, I felt sure the time had come. I climbed high onto the garage roof and leaped off confident that the partridge wings clutched in my six-year-old hands would enable me to soar away. It was my first indication that I was not, after all, omnipotent. I sprained both my ankles and cut my knees.

Memories of my early years are often so obscure that they appear to be half-forgotten dreams, dormant remnants of my childhood sleep. Certainly I know that, as a child, I dreamed of flying or floating through the air, usually wearing exotic costumes. My dreams were all in vital colors, strongly dramatic, very positive, always starring myself. I think the earliest one I can recall is a recurring dream, where I was trying to save some chickens from a fox. Birds and winged creatures featured prominently in those early dreams. Later the accent was on wild, tidal waters and violent currents. Sometimes I have nightmares about huge bird creatures made of sticks. They are seven feet tall and always they are coming across the water to where I try to hide myself beneath the sand.

A Day

5:15 a.m. The alarm rings viciously. It can't be morning yet. I let Lapis out. A few moments alone in the kitchen. Hot fragrant coffee. The day stretches ahead of me. It seems so long.

5:35 a.m. I walk through the empty streets in a somnambulistic state. Extraordinary light patterns in the sky. Ice is on the roads. Strange shadows.

5:45 a.m. I am the first one on the rink. Outside the darkness begins to fade. I trace school figures on the fresh ice sheet. A solitary skater. Images attack my mind. I fight to concentrate.

8:15 a.m. A period of rest. Barely time to go back home but I do so anyway. I sip coffee in the silence and return refreshed.

8:30 a.m. Begin again. More skaters have arrived. We glide past one another wordlessly, each one intent on his own figures.

9-10 a.m. Figure lessons from my trainer. Concentration is intense. The body bends this way and that. Boredom is always at my side. The cold is almost more than I can bear.

11:00 a.m. Time for myself. Precious beyond belief. More than an hour. A choice to be made. Only one thing can be done. Dry cleaning to collect, bank, supplies, letters to be written. I reject them all. They can wait another day. I hurry home again. A time of blessed peace painting undisturbed. Lapis, music — I ask for nothing more. I curse every single phone call.

12:15 p.m. Back to the rink. Gray, shrouded day. Snow seems near.

12:30 p.m. Warm-up on the ice. The first free-skate session, the hardest of the day. Physical agony almost too hard to bear. Constant supervision from my trainer. Training is relentless.

1:30 p.m.	A brief lunch at the club. A bowl of soup and tea. My body aches all over. Muscles scream.
1:45 p.m.	School figures. The body goes through routine motions.
2:45 p.m.	Free-skating. Hard, grinding work, the worst of all. It seems the hour will never end. The five-minute program must be tried again before I leave. I feel I'm going to die.
4:00 p.m.	I leave the club as quickly as I can. Race home for the mail. After all, you never know.
4:05 p.m.	Hunger is gnawing at me. I cook my supper and eat it with Lapis lying on my feet. I feel myself relax.
4:30 p.m.	Almost two hours to paint undisturbed. Time seems to fly — there never is enough. I guard it jealously. Painting is therapeutic, washing away the tensions of the day.
6:15 p.m.	Mrs. Burka returns from the rink. I sit with her and drink a cup of coffee while she has her meal. We discuss the details of the day with care. What has been done, what is still to do, phone calls to be made.
7:00 p.m.	Back to the studio. Painting requires constant application. Hours of careful work. Music.
9:00 p.m.	Another choice to make. I can paint until I go to bed or free-skate once again. I decide to skate. The night is dark and without stars.
9:10 p.m.	The rink is brightly lit. It becomes a different place by night, takes on a new dimension. Skaters stroke around the ice. Mirrored images spin past. I begin to feel elated and my energy returns.
10:15 p.m.	I go home again to paint. The house is quiet and Lapis is asleep. My work progresses smoothly, starts to flow. Abilities are sharpened late at night.
12:00 p.m.	Reluctantly I go to bed. Fatigue sets in. Such ecstasy to crawl between the sheets at last. Supreme luxury to stretch each limb and rest. Sleep comes.

Don't ask me: What about tomorrow? I do not wish to

answer you until today has gone

Sometimes I physically ache with the desire to outdo myself. My head feels as if it would burst and I am consumed by a torrent of energy. A need to create. At other times I am gripped by a supreme inertia, an ultimate lethargy, when I feel nothing nothing nothing.

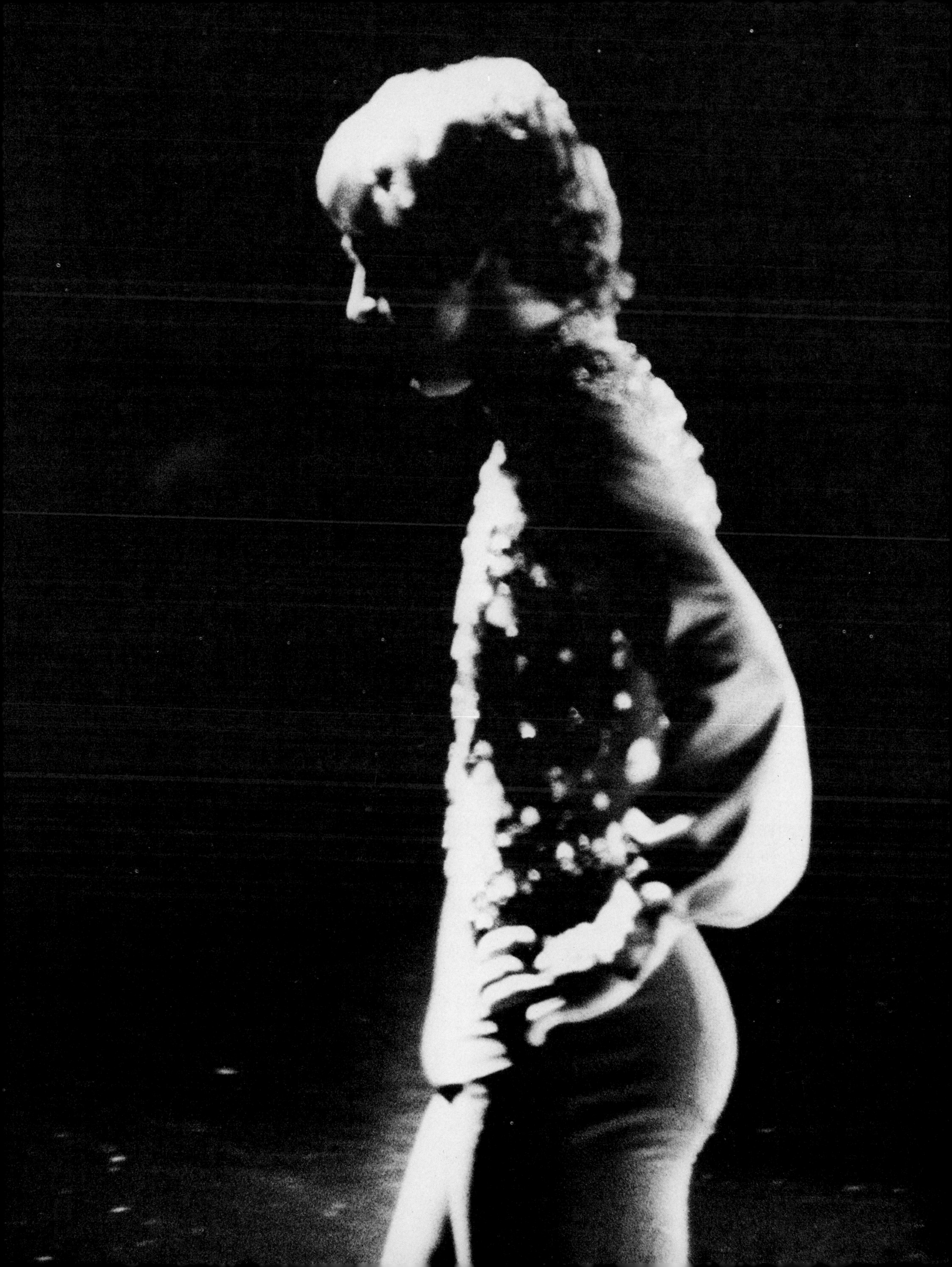

It would be hypocritical of me to say that I am not interested in winning the gold medal, to claim that I don't care. After all, for years I have worked towards it ceaselessly, day in and day out. Of course I want it but my life does not depend upon it. My skating career I value for itself, but what the gold medal amounts to essentially is primitive evidence of success. To win it would mean my views on skating, which are not altogether orthodox, would become globally accepted. I want more than anything to leave an indelible imprint on the face of skating. To give it a whole new direction.

Praise is the lifeblood of a performer, but he must never, never allow himself to believe that praise. Otherwise he might lose the obsession to prove himself again and again. Whenever I go out onto the ice in any major competition, I always think, "Skating well is the best revenge of all." And the adrenalin surges.

I have always regretted the fact that Lawrence Owen died before I could make her acquaintance. I saw her skate in the Olympics in Squaw Valley in 1960, and her skating was so different, so uplifting, she absolutely mesmerized me. She was lit with an inner radiance, a kind of love. What a tragedy that her life ended at sixteen. She was on board the plane bearing the American skating contingent to the World Championships in Prague in 1961. It crashed killing the entire United States team.

I sincerely believe that Janet Lynn is the greatest female skater the world has ever seen. She has had an important influence on skating, and she has a quality about her that almost defies description. She is elfin, wispy, ethereal, mischievous, and inspiring. There is something almost mystical in the way she moves, the flow of her hair, the delicate motion of her arms, the dream-like fluidity. She is a beautiful wraith.

I have a burning compulsion to achieve. To do everything, everywhere. Never to stop moving forward, even for one moment. There is so much to be done, and time is always my enemy.

It was such a relief to have nothing to do but wander from room to room, from one idle pastime to the next letting the days drift past, feeling tension become tranquility. I read and slept and ate and stared into space waiting, without really waiting, to reach the other side of the void. I believe that in that week I hid even from myself. Then, one morning, I awoke with the stirrings of new hope, and I was able to begin again.

A Minute

I have to skate first. Impossible to finish the warm-up. Two minutes to go, and I stand by the boards trying to steel myself for the performance. Emptying my mind. I have to forget everything, everyone. Only the competition exists . . . One minute to go, and I realize with horror that my skates are loose. They need to be tightened. There isn't enough time. My God! What shall I do? I bend over and tear at the laces. Frantic. They're frayed and won't pass through the eyelets. Panic thickens my fingers, renders them useless. I try to force the ends, clawing at them from the other side. My head reels. What can I do? Time is almost up. If I am late on the ice, once my name is called, I am disqualified. Yet to skate in loose boots could mean disaster. Desperation turns my fingers into pincers, and I somehow manage to lace my skates. But they still need tightening. They are still too loose. My name is called. I have no choice. I must go on.

No, Toller has never allowed himself to become involved in the political aspects of skating. He is too much of an idealist for that. And stubborn—my God! No one can make him do something he doesn't believe in. He is interested only in the purest aspects of skating. Simple expertise. Either he is good enough or he isn't. That is the only way he is interested in being judged. Good, better, or best. And I agree with him—one hundred percent. No use in making bargains with talent.

Mrs. Burka

On Losing in Bratislava

I had won the compulsory free-skate and had been properly prepared for the final competition. I had been consistently trained. Yet at the crucial point my nerve gave way—my mental strength left me. I just crawled through my program. It shook me to the very foundations of my soul. I had tasted abject failure. I almost gave up at that point, but I knew in my heart that I couldn't finish my career on that sour note. So I determined that I would compete again. I didn't know if I could skate well in Munich, but I did know that I was going to give it one hell of a try.

On Losing in Colorado

No excuses. I simply didn't do it. When the moment came to perform the chemistry was wrong. I had every chance. I was disappointed, naturally, but with myself, not with the results. My music, Prokofiev's *Cinderella,* was an unwise choice for competition, but it was something I wanted very much to do. For me it was an artistic advance and I still believe in it. It was I, rather than the music, who failed in Colorado.

It was such a relief to have nothing to do but wander from room to room, from one idle pastime to the next letting the days drift past, feeling tension become tranquility. I read and slept and ate and stared into space waiting, without really waiting, to reach the other side of the void. I believe that in that week I hid even from myself. Then, one morning, I awoke with the stirrings of new hope, and I was able to begin again.

Even at her best fame is an elusive lover. She teases, flashing her delicious smile. She affords brief glimpses of her sweetest bounties, promising much more.

Sometimes you think you are running away,
only to find that you are just arriving

There was a young skater named Toller,
Who made people laugh, scream, and holler.
He'd do a mazurka,
For a lady named Burka—
Providing she paid him a dollar.

Genius is a strong word, not to be used lightly. I sincerely believe it applies to the Canadian painter, Gary Slipper. He is without doubt the greatest symbolist painter this country has ever produced. The intellectual content of his paintings is astounding. His work is timeless and has a universal application. He excels in every aspect of his art. His draughtsmanship is unparalleled, his technique is staggering, his composition and subject matter fertile and imaginative.

I first became aware of Gary Slipper's work while I was a student at the Ecole des Beaux Arts. We students would often spend our lunch hours touring the galleries in Montreal and being highly cynical about the things we saw. One day I saw a painting that astonished me—that burned itself into my brain. It was a symbolist painting full of flying people. When I looked around I saw that that there were more. I had found a soul-mate, someone with whom I could communicate. I was thrilled beyond words and knew I had to meet this artist.

Six years later we were both exhibiting at the same gallery, and after the opening we were invited to dinner. I shall always remember meeting Gary. He was such a quiet, gentle man, simple and unimposing. He had old eyes in a young face and did not look like an artist. It was the sensitive hands that betrayed him. He spoke in a low, velvet voice.

"How do you do, Toller?" he said quietly. I had six years of pent-up questions to ask this man, and I asked them all that evening. I must have exhausted him, for he left early.

Not long after that first meeting the gallery closed and Gary disappeared. I found out that he had gone to Vancouver, but nobody knew where he was. In desperation I wrote a letter to the RCMP asking if they knew of his whereabouts. I enclosed a postcard with my name and address on it, simply saying "Gary, please write." Three months later, when I had given up hope of ever hearing from him, I received the strangest letter I had ever seen. It was written in a microscopic hand, as though it had been penned by one of the small people in his paintings. He was in Vancouver. As luck would have it, the Canadian Championships were in Vancouver that year, and we arranged to meet. We talked for many hours, and we discussed the organizing of a group of Mystic Symbolist painters. He returned with me to Toronto and we started the new movement.

An Hour

Six o'clock. An hour still to go. I almost wish it would never pass. Is this shirt all right? I can't decide. Tonight a whole year's work is on trial. Suppose nobody comes except faithful friends? Will I ever be able to convince anybody I'm not just a skater who paints? What about the critics? Will they come? How will they judge my work? Perhaps I've been too close to the paintings. Too subjective. It's possible, yet I'm certain that my work has evolved. Improved. But people may prefer the older style . . . The minutes pass so slowly. This is so different from a performance. I can only wait to be judged. And explain. No, I refuse to explain anything. Everyone must interpret for himself. Every person must relate to the paintings from his own point of view. Suppose nothing sells? How will I ever pay the framer? My hands are trembling. I have never felt so alone and helpless in my life. I feel like phoning somebody. Who? What would I say? What do I expect them to do? No one can help now. Well, I've done my best. I couldn't have worked any harder. I put everything I had into it. Each painting has a little piece of my soul in it. I have to stand behind them. By eleven tonight I'll know what other people think. My God, how slowly the seconds are ticking past. Creeping forward. Whatever happens, I have to look relaxed, confident. I have to generate enthusiasm.

It must be every child's dream to represent his country in the Olympics. It was certainly a dream I had savored all my life. When I failed to make the Canadian team in Vancouver in 1968, my hopes were dashed to pieces on the ice. Four more years seemed too long to wait. I felt there could never be another chance but I was wrong. In 1972 I did, in fact, make the Olympic team, and I stepped inside the aura of the dream. My goal was reached. But the long-awaited spectacle was an anti-climax. The Olympic mystique was shattered by the crass realities of the Games. The real superstars were the members of the media, not the athletes. The figure skaters, who were competing at the very end of the Games, had only three quarters of an hour each day for practice, which made it very difficult to improve. All we could do was coast and hope to hold on to the level we had already achieved. Few performances did any credit to the skaters. For the first time in my life I was not particularly proud to be a part of the skating contingent, and when a stranger in the crowd asked me what I was, I unhesitatingly told him I was a bobsledder.

Had I not become a skater I think I might well have made a mark in diving. The possibilities for creative diving are still totally unexplored. There are boundless opportunities for innovation. Diving now is still a purely physical sport, but imagine what would happen if one added emotion to the dives. Profound statements could be made in those split seconds in the air. The logical progression of artistic diving would inevitably lead to pair diving, which would be the only way to express true love and outright war. Then the choreographers would come, and it would all culminate with Theatre-in-the-Air. And what fantastic costumes one could wear! Maybe I'll do it yet. After all, one is never too old to dive.

The older I get, the more I realize that the greatest force in my life is my work. It is the only thing I can rely on completely. Time, therefore, is of vital importance to me. I have the most dreadful hangups about it. If I take the time to do anything which is outside the general pattern of my life, I am immediately seized by a strong sense of guilt. I feel always as though time is against me—as if I were racing death to the finish line. Yet to be totally organized must be anti-creative, for how do you know—how can you possibly *know*—that the next road you wander down, the next face you take time to gaze into won't stir in you a new beginning?

Performers are like chefs. Their role is to bake fantastic, exotic desserts to present to the public, but they must never, never save even the smallest piece for themselves.

The basis of all art is sincerity. To be yourself, to rely on your own judgement, your own gut feeling of what is right. The thing I personally value above everything, even technique, is concept. To be a genuine individualist requires a great deal of strength and courage. It is never easy to chart new territory, to cross new frontiers, or to introduce subtle shadings to an established color.

In skating the difference between a great performance and a mediocre performance is primarily a matter of conviction. The skater must make the audience believe in him as fiercely as he believes in himself. It isn't a question of how many triple jumps he can land or how many times he falls. What really counts is the total overall impression he leaves behind. The degree of personal involvement.

Moments before — heart beats too fast — nerves tighten — mind races — conscious effort to relax — to block out thought — to become weak — controlled tingling spreads through every limb — confidence mounts — the audience is far away — mind's eye focuses — body waits — the sculptor has become the sculpture — electricity begins to pulse — energy diffuses — hot liquid steel — music explodes — into the Fourth Dimension — time stops — reality ceases to exist — inside the sanctuary music forms the walls — skating is like dreams — moving like water, air and wind — body cutting space — exploring angles — spirit without inhibition — reaching out to catch the star — chasing the tail of the dream — the dream is broken — only shattered fragments fill the air — but every soul must be embraced — the final statement must be understood — skating is a language beyond words.

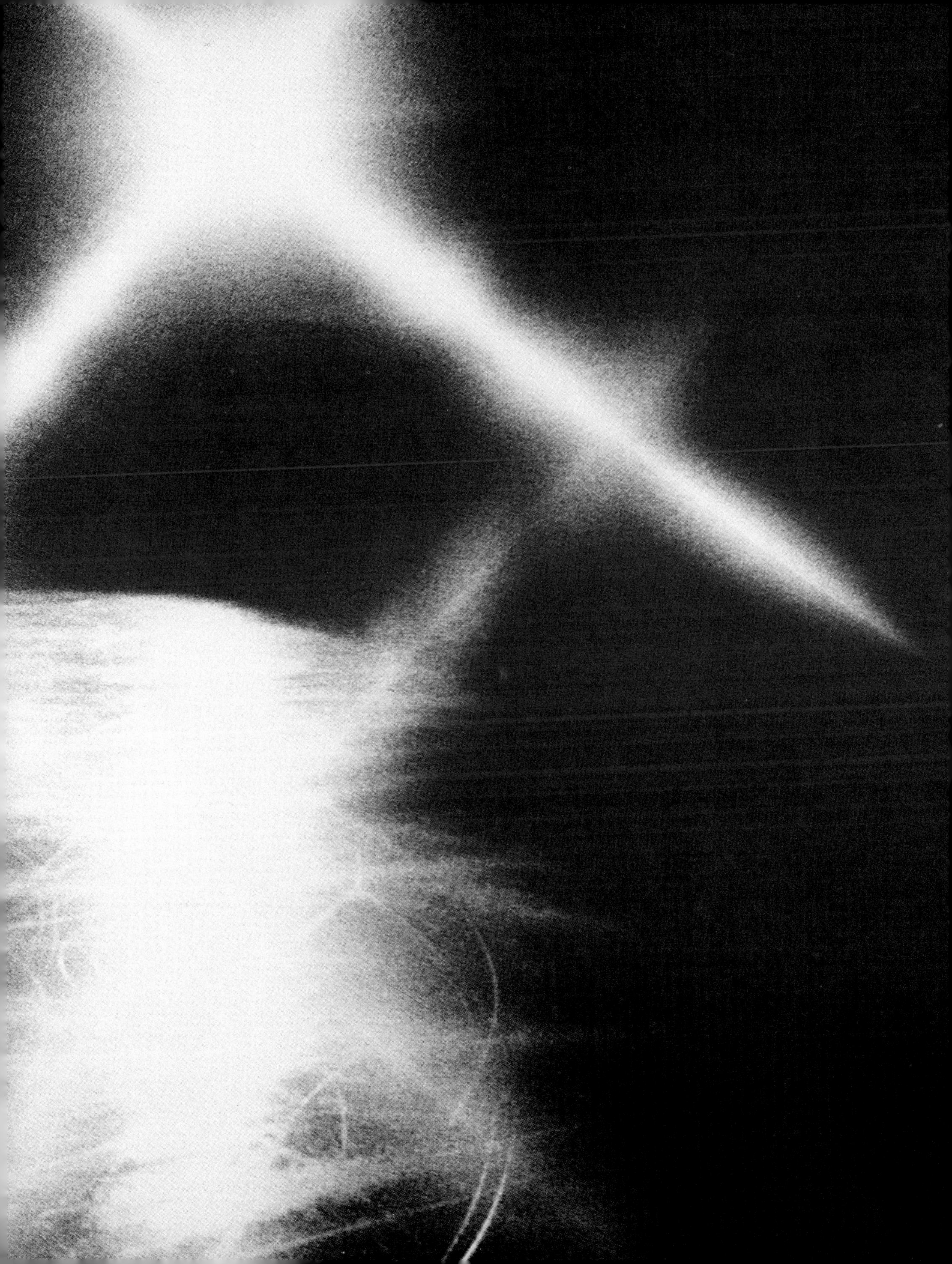

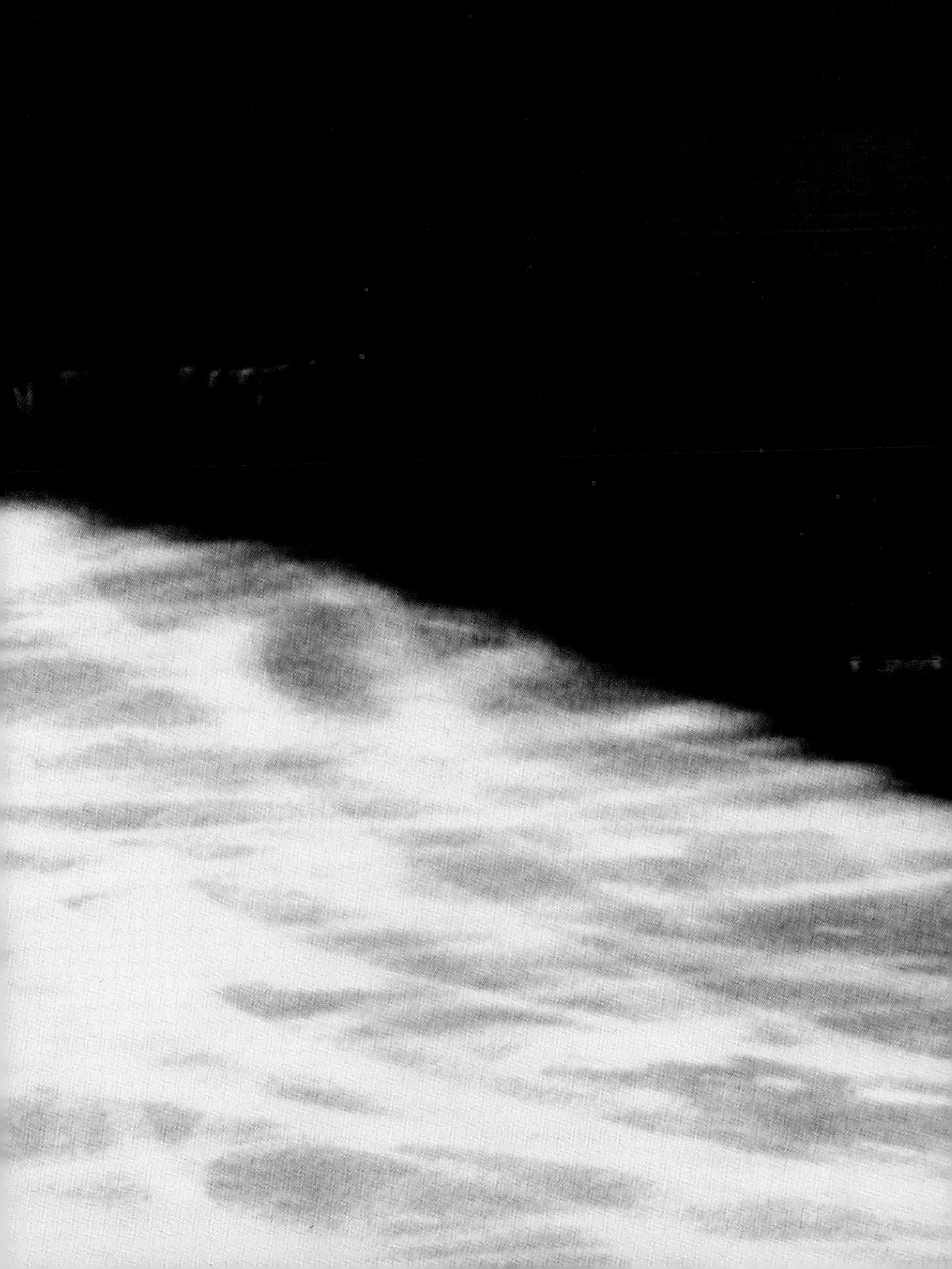

Human potential stops at a point somewhere beyond infinity